23 LOST AT SEA

WRITTEN BY

JENNIFER KLOCKEMAN

ILLUSTRATED BY

MARK LUDY

First Printing
September 2011

Whimsical Ways Publishing
www.WhimsicalWaysPublishing.com

Klockeman, Jennifer.
Ludy, Mark.
23 Lost at Sea/Jennifer Klockeman; illustrations by Mark Ludy. 1st Ed.
p. cm.
Summary: Twenty-three artists get shipwrecked amongst a group of islands that look like paradise. Much to their dismay, each is stranded on a separate island patrolled by an enormous sea monster. Alone and held captive on their own island, they long for each other's company. One day, an artist begins to build a bridge. This idea takes hold and soon all the artists are together again. Still they must all face their biggest fear, the sea monster. Working together, they discover the true meaning of paradise, and it is not where you live or how you live, but how you embrace those who live with you.

Library of Congress Control Number: 2011927035
ISBN 978-0-9835275-0-3

Printed in USA

To God for His miracles,
Mom for her constant support,
Courtney for her time and skills,
Summer for the inspiration, and
David for putting up with a rhyming woman.

- Jennifer Klockeman

On a warm sunny day
on a boat in the bay,
twenty-three artists went sailing away.

They left full of hope;
they left with a cheer,
there were even a few who left with a tear.

There were those who could paint,
some who could draw,
others could sew,
while some carved with a saw.

There were those who could sing,
while some sculpted in clay.
Quite a few liked to write;
others put on a play.

LIFE SAVER

Around the world they planned to sail,

to see great sights, perhaps a whale!

The pyramids, the rain forest, Mount Kilimanjaro,

a solar eclipse predicted tomorrow.

Some worked all night, some worked all day;

to most their work felt more like play.

Inspired by such magnificent sights,

each felt their work was reaching new heights.

One night dark clouds came rolling in,
with that came rain and then the wind.
Soon the waves began to swell,
the artists were not feeling well.

The boat dove up, the boat dove down,
pitched side to side and round and round.
At last the boat got pitched so high
it went straight up into the sky.

It landed where no one has been,

or ever will be seen again.

It landed with a great big splash

then fell to pieces from the crash.

Yet on the pieces of the boat,

each artist clung to stay afloat.

The wind had died, the rain was gone,

the stars were out, the sea was calm.

Amid the darkness of the night,
a group of islands came to sight.
A place like this they'd never seen.
was it for real, or just a dream?

Soon artists paddled, kicked, and swam
to reach the closest piece of land.
Appearing divided by the sea,
each artist quickly climbed a tree.

Now in full view
each heart did sink,
for no two islands
had a link.

The days ahead they waved and shouted,
some sat down and even pouted.

Until one artist who liked to swim
jumped in the ocean on a whim.
But as he swam he saw a sight
that struck in him a terrible fright.

Another artist planned to float
to his neighbor's on a boat.
A boat he patched that very day,
until he too was scared away.

Stuck on their islands all alone,

with lots of time each built a home.

The homes they built came in all shapes and sizes,

no two looked alike; each was full of surprises.

Each special home had a magical view,

so why weren't they happy? Not even a few?

Well, happiness, you see,
is much better when shared.
Without one another,
all were lonely, some scared.

Soon each one's heart
had started to ache,
if kept apart,
they surely would break.

Until one day
there came a thought:
a bridge, of course!
A bridge, why not!

And so that artist
began his plight.
He worked all day
into the night.

Others watched
and scratched their heads,
blew out their lights
and went to bed.

In the morning,
in the light,
the artists woke
to quite a sight.

On one island
now stood two,
hugging, smiling,
no longer blue!

Soon the artists,
hammers in hand,
were building bridges
from land to land.

One artist helped
by playing the fiddle.
Most of them worked
till they met in the middle.

They gathered to celebrate, to have a great feast,

when who should swim by but the **big bad beast**.

At last they could speak what had been on their minds;

they'd all feared this creature by now for some time.

Now the face of the beast had yet to be seen,
still all had imagined it ghastly and mean.
They pictured sharp teeth, eyes black and hollow,
a mouth that breathed fire would toast you, then swallow.
How could they catch it? What could they do?
Would it roast them alive and chew them in two?

Then came a plan
from an artist who knit.
She'd knit them a net,
in which the beast fit.

They'd catch him
and hoist him out of the ocean.
What they'd do next
she hadn't a notion.

The cook suggested they have a great feast.

Perhaps a contest, who'd eat the most beast!

She could make beast soup or a tender beast roast;

she could make beast stew or beast gravy on toast!

And so came the day when the net had been knit.
They all eyed the beast, most sure it would fit.

To their amazement, the beast swam straight in!
The artists all cheered at the luck of their win.

Then in the thick net they hoisted him high,
until with the beast they stood eye to eye.

Most stood back, afraid to look.
Some closed their eyes, while others shook.

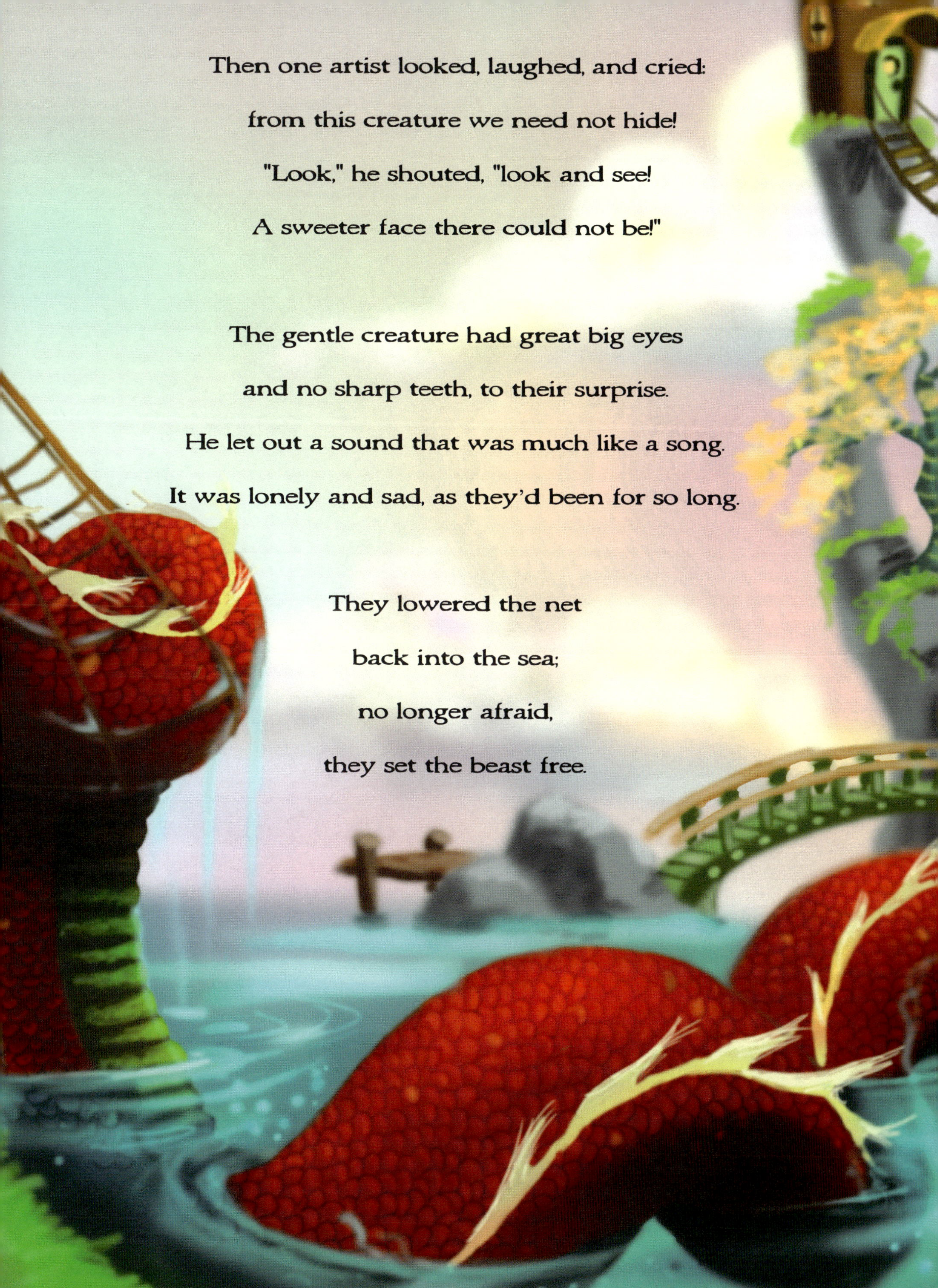

Then one artist looked, laughed, and cried:
from this creature we need not hide!
"Look," he shouted, "look and see!
A sweeter face there could not be!"

The gentle creature had great big eyes
and no sharp teeth, to their surprise.
He let out a sound that was much like a song.
It was lonely and sad, as they'd been for so long.

They lowered the net
back into the sea;
no longer afraid,
they set the beast free.

They began to boat,

they began to swim;

they plunged in the ocean

by just diving in.

Soon their new friend

swam by their sides;

before very long

he was giving them rides.

Laughing and chatting,

happy as could be,

now twenty-four strangers

were friends in the sea.

AUTHOR - Jennifer Klockeman

Jennifer Klockeman and her husband of 30 years have two grown daughters. She loves animals, nature, children, the elderly and the outdoors and is an avid quilter. This is her first book and she hopes it encourages people of all ages to reach out and connect to one another. Learn more at KLOCKEMAN.com.

ILLUSTRATOR - Mark Ludy

Is the author and illustrator of several beloved books such as "The Flower Man", "The Farmer", "JuJo" and "The Grump" and a regular speaker. He as well is the director of The Giving Artist, a non-profit devoted to impacting the lives of the orphan, widow and poor through art. Learn how you can get involved.

Every book purchased is an act of GIVING 10%

Learn more at: MarkLudy.com & TheGivingArtist.org

"A Miracle for Summer"

Miracles, do they still happen today? This children's story was created alongside a quilt I made, pictured on the back of this book, which was inspired by a true miracle that happened to our family in 2003.

At 19, our older daughter, Summer, contracted the West Nile virus from mosquito bites while camping. That year, West Nile was an epidemic in Colorado. Although most people who caught it just got flu-like symptoms, others suffered complications from extreme fatigue all the way to death. Summer ended up catching Meningitis and Encephalitis from it and lay in a medically induced coma in ICU hooked up to 13 IV bags and on a respirator, for she had gone into acute respiratory distress. She then became septic. The last straw was when she ironically received a blood transfusion carrying the same West Nile virus that had put her in the hospital in the first place. This was before they knew about the incubation period of the disease in the blood. Needless to say, we were overcome by the staggering odds against her survival, as any one of these things alone could kill her. Altogether, it appeared to be a death sentence.

One morning on the way to ICU, a woman I'd noticed standing outside the ICU for days stopped me. She asked if I knew who she was. I thought perhaps I recognized her from church, but in a church of ten thousand people, it was hard to say. She introduced herself as Karen, and said she was on the prayer team at our church. She went on to tell me that God had placed Summer on her heart. She'd been standing out there, this total stranger, praying for our daughter all this time and we weren't even aware of it.

She asked me to coffee in the hospital cafeteria. There she proceeded to tell me that God had a message for me and I could take it or leave it. She said, "You are going to receive bad news tomorrow." I replied, "I get Summer's MRI results from her brain scan tomorrow." These were her next words. "If you choose to believe the doctor tomorrow, it will happen. If you choose to claim healing in the name of the Lord, it will happen. The choice is yours." I thanked her for her message and really didn't know quite what to make of it.

The following day, the neurologist's exact words to us as he held the MRI were, "This is horrible ... horrible." He told us that Summer had such massive brain damage that she no longer had a brain stem and her brain looked like that of a person who had suffered twenty strokes. He went on to say if she woke up at all, we would need to find a facility that could give her full time care. In essence, our 19 year old would live in an elderly home and never be able to do anything for herself again. The news could not have been more devastating! Since my dad was a pathologist, my normal response would have been to believe and accept this neurologist's word as our daughter's fate.

Then Karen's words came back to me. I walked away from the doctor rejecting what he had told me. Some would call it denial, but I was consciously choosing to believe in someone wiser than any doctor. Someone I knew existed from past experience... God.

I went into Summer's room where my husband and a nurse were, and began thinking of some verses I knew from the bible that God promised. One I knew was He promised a future. I told Him I'd rather He take her from us than her have the future the doctor described. I didn't believe that was the future the bible promised. I knew God promised that He could turn even the worse situations into good for those who loved Him, and I had witnessed Him do it countless times in my own life and others. He also promised that whenever two or more were gathered in His name, they would be heard by Him and answered. We knew there were hundreds, possibly a thousand, gathered around the world praying on her behalf, and the bible says it only takes two. I knew, of course, that sometimes God's answers to your prayers are "no"....for reasons we may not understand and find hard to except and that we must all die sometime. I simply refused to believe this was her time. I claimed those promises out loud and told God I was holding Him to them and believing Him for them.

The next day, Summer opened an eye. Eventually she could blink responses, so we knew she was indeed in there. While in the hospital she had to relearn to sit, walk with a walker, speak, and feed herself.

After leaving the hospital 38 days from when she entered, she had over 3 months of physical, speech and eye therapy. Amazingly she was able to return to college the next semester. At her sixth month check-up, her neurologist was amazed to see her walk into his office, with no signs of what she had been through other than a tracheotomy scar. He had no explanation for the new MRI he held in his hand that showed a full brain stem and a brain with only one little spot of damage to it.

Summer now teaches the third grade and is getting married this summer. Now that's a future to look forward to!! Thanks be to God!!

So if you find yourself or a loved one faced with insurmountable odds of any nature, remember four things: 1) You are not alone. There is a God who loves you. 2) To find Him, you only need to seek Him earnestly and open your heart. 3) Miracles still do happen! 4) Man, no matter who he is, doesn't have the last word. God does. So don't lose hope!

- Jennifer Klockeman, 2011

9855560R0003

Made in the USA
Charleston, SC
19 October 2011